Look After Yourself

Healthy Skin

Angela Royston

Heinemann Library
Chicago, Illinois

© 2003 Heinemann Library
a division of Reed Elsevier Inc.
Chicago, Illinois

Designed by Dave Oakley
Photo research by Helen Reilly
Originated by Dot Gradations Ltd
Printed and bound in China by South China Printing Company

07 06 05 04 03
10 9 8 7 6 5 4 3 2 1

Library of Congress Cataloging-in-Publication Data
Royston, Angela.
  Healthy skin / Angela Royston.
      v. cm. -- (Look after yourself)
Includes bibliographical references and index.
Contents: Your body -- What is skin? -- What else does skin do? -- Taking
care of your skin -- Keeping your skin clean -- Drying your skin -- Watch out
for warts! -- Dry skin -- Cover up in the sun -- Using sunscreen -- Cuts -- Scabs
 -- It's a fact!
  ISBN 1-4034-4444-7 (libr. bdg.) -- ISBN 1-4034-4453-6 (pbk.)
  1. Skin--Juvenile literature. 2. Skin--Care and hygiene--Juvenile literature.
[1. Skin. 2. Skin--Care and hygiene.] I. Title.
  QP88.5.R688 2003
  646.7'26--dc21
                              2003000997

Acknowledgments
The author and publisher are grateful to the following for permission to reproduce copyright material:
Cover photograph by David Schmidt/Masterfile.
p. 4 Kaz Mori/Getty Images; pp. 5, 11, 15, 19, 21, 23, 24, 25 Trevor Clifford; pp. 6, 8 Powerstock; p. 7 Leslie McFarland/Trip; p. 9 Colin Hawkins/Getty Images; p. 10 Bananastock; p. 12 Laura Lane; pp. 13, 14, 17 Martin Sookias; p. 16 Dr. Jeremy Burgess/Science Photo Library; p. 18 Inc. Janeart; p. 20 Laurent Delhourbe; p. 22 Aja Productions; p. 26 Pascal Carpet; p. 27 Angela Hampton/Bubbles.

Special thanks to David Wright for his help in the preparation of this book.

Some words are shown in bold, **like this.** You can find out what they mean by looking in the glossary.

Contents

Your Body

Your body is like a machine. It has many different parts that work together. Each part of your body has a special job to do.

Skin covers your whole body.
It separates your insides
from the outside world.

What Is Skin?

Skin is made up of two main layers. The **epidermis** is the top layer of skin. Your epidermis is thin, but tough.

The layer under that is called the **dermis.** It contains **melanin.** Melanin protects your skin from the sun. People with pale skin only have a little melanin. People with dark skin have lots of melanin.

Skin is **waterproof.** When you swim, water cannot seep through your skin into your body. Skin also stops the inside of your body from drying out.

8

Most of your skin is covered with fine hairs.
These hairs help keep your body warm.
When you are too hot, your skin **sweats**
to cool you down.

Skin is tough. You can cover it with face paint and then wash the paint off. You need to take care of your skin to keep it healthy.

You will soon know if your skin becomes unhealthy. It will start to itch or become sore. It may also become dry and flaky.

Keeping Your Skin Clean

You need to wash your skin to keep it healthy.
Soap helps to remove dirt and dried **sweat.**
Make sure you rinse all the soap off your skin.

You should have a shower before and after you swim in a swimming pool. A **chemical** in the water called **chlorine** can make your skin dry and itchy. A shower washes it off.

Drying Your Skin

Dry your skin with a clean towel. Make sure you dry yourself all over, especially between your toes. **Talcum powder** helps to get your skin really dry.

If your feet are often damp or **sweaty,** the skin between your toes may become itchy and flaky. This is called **athlete's foot.** It can be cured with a special powder.

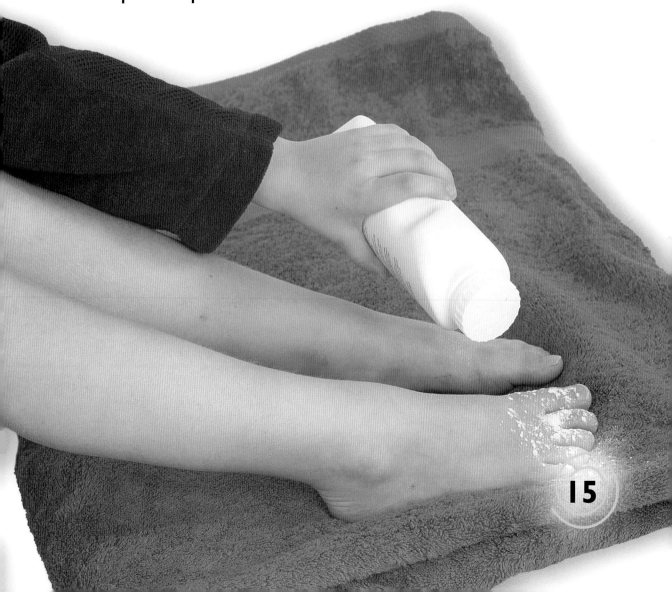

Watch out for Warts!

A wart is a small patch or bump on your skin. Warts are caused by a **virus.** People can get warts on their hands and feet.

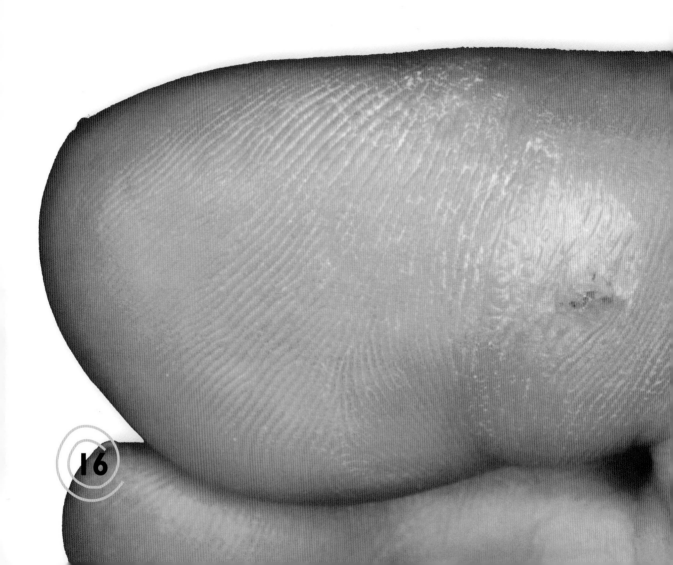

You can catch warts from other people, but it does not happen very easily. You can get rid of warts with special **medicines.** If you do have a wart on your foot, you should keep it covered.

Dry Skin

Your skin may become dry and itchy if you spend a lot of time in heated rooms. Cold, windy weather can also make your skin dry out.

You can use skin cream or lotion to make dry skin feel better, or to stop your skin from drying out. Rub the cream into your skin.

Cover Up in the Sun

The Sun's rays can harm your skin. When it is hot and sunny, wear clothing that will **protect** the skin on your back, chest, head, and arms.

A hat can shade your face from the sun's rays. If your hair is short, it is a good idea to make sure that the back of your neck is covered, too.

Using Sunscreen

Sunscreen stops the sun from burning your skin. Put it on before you go outside. Rub in more cream after an hour or two, or after you have been swimming.

Sunscreen bottles have a number on them.
Sunscreen with a high number lets you stay in
the sun longer than sunscreen with a low number.

People with dark skin need to use sunscreen, too. Even if you put on sunscreen, you should still wear a shirt and hat.

Cuts

Skin normally keeps **germs** out of your body. But if your skin is scratched or broken, germs can get in. Blood helps wash germs out of a cut.

You can help your body keep out germs. Wash a scratch in clean water. If a cut or scratch is bleeding, cover it with a clean bandage.

Scabs

After a while, a hard **scab** forms over a cut or scratch. The scab **protects** the **wound** while new skin grows. When new skin has formed, the scab falls off.

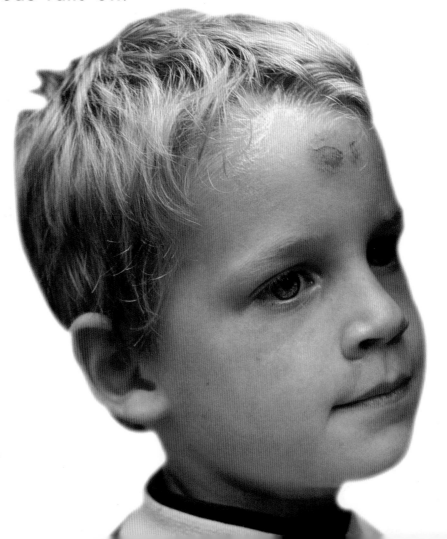

26

Do not pick scabs. Wait for them to fall off on their own. If you pull off a scab too soon, the cut may start to bleed again.

It's a Fact!

Your skin contains tiny **pores** that allow **sweat** to come out of your body. Most of your skin has up to 100 sweat pores for every half inch square (about one cm). That is an area about the same size as your big toenail!

Some parts of your skin contain more sweat pores than other parts. The skin on the palms of your hands and on the **soles** of your feet has a lot of sweat pores. It is important to wash your hands and feet to remove dried sweat.

The top layer of your skin is made of tiny flakes of dead skin. Washing helps to remove the dead skin. Millions of these flakes rub off every day. In fact, most of the dust in your home is made up of flakes of skin!

Pale skin burns more easily than skin that contains a lot of **melanin.** People with pale skin have to be especially careful to protect their skin from the sun.

Some people have **eczema.** Patches of their skin become very dry and itchy. Special cream can help make the skin less dry. Eczema cannot be passed from one person to another.

You may sometimes get a **rash** on your skin. Your skin becomes red and covered with small spots. Many different things can cause a rash. An **allergy** to something, such as a food or soap, can cause a rash. Some illnesses, such as chicken pox and scarlet fever, also cause a rash.

Glossary

allergy   reaction, such as itching or sneezing, by a person's body to things that do not bother other people, such as animal hair, dust, or flowers

athlete's foot   disease that makes the skin between toes itchy and flaky

chemical   substance, for example chlorine, which is put into the water of swimming pools

chlorine   chemical that is added to the water in swimming pools to kill germs

dermis   layer of skin under the epidermis that holds hair, oil, and blood

eczema   patch of very dry, itchy skin

epidermis   tough, outer layer of skin that you can touch and see

germ   tiny living thing that attacks different parts of the body; a germ can cause sickness

medicine   substance used to treat a sickness

melanin brown chemical in the skin that protects you
  from the harmful rays of the sun
pore small opening in the skin
protect to keep safe
rash many small red spots on the skin
scab dried blood that makes a hard covering over
  a cut or scratch
sole underside of a foot
sweat salty water that the body makes in the skin
talcum powder white powder that contains perfume
  and that people put on after bathing
virus type of germ that can easily pass to other people
waterproof does not allow water to pass through
wound cut or scratch

More Books to Read

Royston, Angela. *Chicken Pox.* Chicago: Heinemann
  Library, 2001.
Royston, Angela. *Clean and Healthy.* Chicago:
  Heinemann Library, 1999.
Maurer, Tracy. *Skin.* Vero Beach, Fla.: Rourke
  Publishing, 1999.

Index